CUCUMBER CURTIS
CAN'T COME TO DINNER

COPYRIGHT © 2021 BRAD GOSSE
IMAGES COURTESY
VECTORTOONS.COM

ALL RIGHTS RESERVED.

ISBN: 9798510103373

IT ALL BEGINS AT THE GROCERY STORE

THEY HAVE APPLES AND BEER

BANANAS AND MORE

MEET CUCUMBER CURTIS
HE LOVES TO DAY DREAM

OF SALADS

AND SUSHI

AND DRESSINGS WITH CREAM

CURTIS CAN'T WAIT TO COME HOME WITH YOU

OR YOU?

OR YOU?

OR WHAT ABOUT YOU?

THE DAY'S ALMOST OVER
CURTIS STARTS TO FEEL SAD

"NOBODY WANTS ME!"

HE'LL BECOME A PICKLE BEFORE HE GOES BAD

BUT WAIT THERE'S A MOM

EVERYTHING WILL BE FINE

CURTIS IS DANCING THROUGH THE CHECKOUT LINE

HE'S FINALLY GOING HOME TO END HIS SHORT LIFE

AND FULFILL HIS DESTINY WITH YOUR KITCHEN KNIFE

BUT WE WON'T SEE CURTIS AT DINNER TONIGHT

FIRST HE MUST MAKE MOMMY SCREAM WITH DELIGHT

GET YOUR VERY OWN DEAD BABIES BOOKS AND MERCHANDISE

Stickers Just $1

Dead Babies are the hottest thing this Christmas season. Every kid wants a book, sticker and shower curtain. Collect them all or trade with your friends. Digital (NFT) collectables also available.

Order while supplies last.

Only $10 — BOOKS

Satisfaction Guaranteed

CONJOINED TWINS
Where Does One End and The Other Begin?

What if one can swim and the other can not? Can just one of them become an astronaut? How often do they need a diaper change? If they grew 100 feet tall wouldn't that be strange? Are they a by-product of nuclear radiation? Have they ever been left outside a fire station?

LEARN ABOUT INBREEDING WITH DONKEYBEAR

Are your parents cousins or siblings? This book will teach you all about inbreeding. You can learn along with Donkeybear. He's hearing about it for the first time.

MERCHANDISE
bradgosse.redbubble.com

BOOKS
amazon.com/author/bradgosse

Brad Gosse

STD'S & YOU
Learning From The Animals At The Zoo

Meet Hammers The Herpes Hamster. He's one of the many infected animals waiting to teach you about sexually transmitted diseases.

BAA BAA BLACK SHEEP
Deals With Another Routine Stop

Only $10

Baa baa black sheep please step out of the car. Yes sir yes sir please know I'm unarmed. Do you know why I stopped you today?. "Because of the fur color I display?". You match the description of a suspect I seek. Funny it's the 4th time to happen this week. I profiled you because you are black. And you drive a Mercedes which seems kinda whack.

MOMS ONLYFANS
New Beginnings From Difficult Choices

Dad left your mom broke. Now she's faced with the harsh reality of not having enough money. But don't worry she has a plan to get back on her feet.

MERCHANDISE
bradgosse.redbubble.com

BOOKS
amazon.com/author/bradgosse

Does Anyone Know Whatever Happened To
MURDER HORNETS

Remember Murder Hornets? Whatever happened to them? We dive deeply into the terror phenomenon that never came to be. 2020 had so many bigger things, so Murder Hornets were forgotten.

Make Your Own Luck

What can pimps and divorce lawyers teach children, about money and luck? This book tells the story of outdated wisdom and harsh truths.

Cockroach-baby smells really musky. Centipede baby was sewn from human skin. Squid-fish lives deep down in the sea. Flesh-eating ladybug is super scary. Bearded baby was born this hairy.

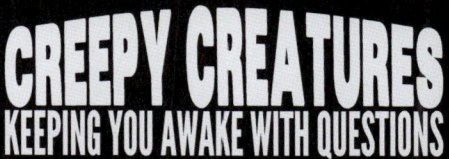

CREEPY CREATURES
KEEPING YOU AWAKE WITH QUESTIONS

STICKERS

Do you like...
CHEESE

MERCHANDISE
bradgosse.redbubble.com

BOOKS
amazon.com/author/bradgosse

OURS BABY
The Only Child Your Step Mom Loves

Your stepmom wants one thing from your dear old dad. Viable sperm and an empty house. Pack your bags it's time to grow up.

MOMMY GOT A DUI

Your mom has secrets. She hides her drinking from you… Until now. Mommy can't drive you to school and you're going to have to learn the bus routes.

INSOMNIAC & FRIENDS
The Clowns That Put You To Sleep

Yeetyeet likes to watch you sleep. Pickles under your bed he creeps. Switchblade eats your favorite stuffies. Pedo lures you away with puppies. Shifty plans to collect your teeth. Twisty smells your hair while you sleep. Clammy lives inside his van. Hank once had to kill a man. Tooty smells your dirty socks. Busby laughs at electric shocks. Twinkles spends the night robbing graves. Fappy keeps a few human slaves.

MY RACIST GRAN

WHY DADDY HITS MOMMY

A Kids Guide To Understanding Alcoholism

MERCHANDISE
bradgosse.redbubble.com

BOOKS
amazon.com/author/bradgosse

Brad Gosse

TRIGGERED
Kids Guide To Cancel Culture

Easily offended is the new trend. People act outraged. Be careful, you might lose your job. Even though nobody is responsible for the feelings of others.

OK BOOMER

Boomer always complains at the store. But it was on sale yesterday!! When yesterday's special isn't available anymore. You shouldn't be such a slut. Boomer gives unsolicited advice. This smart phone is dumber than dirt. Boomer always struggles with his device. Boomer demands your supervisor.

MERCHANDISE
bradgosse.redbubble.com

BOOKS
amazon.com/author/bradgosse

CINNAMON

A horse forced into the sex trade.

Only $10

DON'T BATHE WITH UNCLE JOE
Setting Boundaries With Adults

Uncle Joe lost his job. For misconduct in the workplace. He's coming to stay with us. You're going to have to learn to avoid his hands and more importantly. NEVER bathe with uncle Joe.

Only $10

THIRST TRAPS
Why Moms Phone Keeps Blowing Up

DADDY'S A SIMP
Don't Expect Much Inheritance

MERCHANDISE
bradgosse.redbubble.com

BOOKS
amazon.com/author/bradgosse

Brad Gosse

Printed in Great Britain
by Amazon